For Leni and Harriet.

A SEMI-COMPLETE SURVEY OF NEW YORK CITY AR-
CHITECTURAL TYPOLOGIES AND STYLISTIC
MOVEMENTS, FOR BABIES

Lucas Posada

Copyright © 2022 Lucas Posada

All rights reserved. No part of this book may be reproduced or transmitted in any form or by any means whatsoever without express written permission from the author, except in the case of brief quotations embodied in critical articles and reviews.

ISBN: 9798846413085

A SEMI-COMPLETE SURVEY OF NEW YORK CITY ARCHITECTURAL TYPOLOGIES AND STYLISTIC MOVEMENTS FOR BABIES

OLD CUTIES

or...

NEO-CLASSICAL

FEDERAL HALL,
ALEXANDER JACKSON DAVIS

TRIANGLY ONES

or...

RENAISSANCE REVIVAL

FLATIRON BUILDING, DANIEL BURNHAM

POINTY SPIKERS

OR...

GOTHIC REVIVAL

TRINITY CHURCH,
RICHARD UPJOHN

LACEY-LOUS

OR...

ART NOUVEAU

LITTLE SINGER BUILDING,
ERNEST FLAGG

CAKES

or...

CAST IRON

HAUGHWOUT BUILDING,
J.P. GAYNOR

FANCY-PANTSY

or...

BEAUX-ARTS

NEW YORK PUBLIC LIBRARY,
CARRÈRE + HASTINGS

BELLISIMO

or...

ITALIANATE

BOUWERIE LANE THEATRE,
HENRY ENGELBERT

SPARKLY!

or...

ART DECO

CHRYSLER BUILDING,
WILLIAM VAN ALEN

VERY SERIOUS

or...

BRUTALISM.

MET BREUER,
MARCEL BREUER

KINDA FUNNY

OR...

POST MODERN

AT&T BUILDING,
PHILIP JOHNSON AND JOHN BURGEE

FOLDY FOLDY

OR

DECONSTRUCTIVISM

COOPER UNION NEW ACADEMIC BUILDING, MORPHOSIS

DADDY'S OFFICE ♥

OR...

INTERNATIONAL STYLE

SEAGRAM BUILDING
MIES VAN DER RHOE

Made in United States
North Haven, CT
06 September 2023

41183790R00018